CAESAR TO CHURCHILL
Book One

The Early Years
(400 B.C.—A.D. 1154)

CAESAR TO CHURCHILL

Duncan M. White
M.A., Dip.Ed.

Drawings by P. E. Cleator

ROY PUBLISHERS, INC.
New York 10021

© Duncan M. White 1968

Library of Congress Catalog Number 69–12582

PRINTED IN GREAT BRITAIN

CONTENTS

chapter		page
1	The Ancient World, and Rome	7
2	Ancient and Roman Britain	13
3	Roman Britain and the Destruction of the Empire	20
4	The Coming of the Anglo-Saxons	25
5	The Early Church	33
6	The Coming of the Vikings	39
7	Alfred of Wessex	45
8	The Last Kings of Wessex	52
9	The Norman Conquest	58
10	The First Norman Kings	66
11	The Last Norman Kings	74
12	The Story So Far	81
	When It Happened	84
	Kings of Wessex and England	85

To Brook House

THE ANCIENT WORLD, AND ROME

1

356 B.C.—323 B.C. Life of Alexander the Great
216 B.C. Hannibal's invasion of Rome
44 B.C. Murder of Julius Caesar

The earliest men about whom anything is known lived in caves. Later they began to wander about the earth looking for good land on which to graze their animals. They built themselves huts to live in and soon there were groups of people living together in villages of huts. These villages grew into towns, especially if they were near rivers, for rivers were the best ways of travelling about in those days. The people lived

A stone-age man

in these towns and farmed the countryside around them. In time the towns grew into big cities which ruled the land around them for miles.

There were many such cities in Ancient Greece, but the two most important ones were Sparta and Athens. Sparta was a very strong and warlike city and her army was the best in Greece. Athens was quite different: her citizens preferred learning to fighting, though she had a very good navy. Athens was famous for her wisdom and for the beauty of her buildings. Some of her buildings, such as the Parthenon, an early temple, can still be seen today. Sparta and Athens, however, were rivals and finally Sparta attacked and destroyed Athens at the end of a long war.

A Greek warrior

Sparta, however, did not have long to enjoy her victory, for soon afterwards King Philip of Macedonia, a country to the north of Sparta, invaded and conquered Greece. When Philip died his son Alexander became king. He was perhaps the greatest general who ever lived. He attacked the powerful Persian Empire and conquered in a very short time a huge empire for Macedonia before he died of a fever in 323 B.C. His tremendous conquests earned him the title Alexander the Great.

Had Alexander lived a little later, he would have been faced with a new powerful city growing up to the west of his empire, the city of Rome. The Romans had a strange fable of how their city began, and, although a fable is not really true, this one is very interesting. For ten years, so the story goes, the Greeks had been attacking a city called Troy, without being able to capture it. They decided to try a trick and so built a huge hollow wooden horse in which they hid some soldiers. They then left the horse outside Troy, got into their boats and pretended to sail away. The Trojans were fooled by this and came out to see the strange horse the Greeks had left behind. Thinking it was a Greek god, they pulled it into their city to show the rest of their people, but once inside the walls the Greek soldiers stole out of the horse at night and forced open the city gates to let in the Greek army, which had quietly sailed back. Troy was completely destroyed, but a few of her citizens, led by Aeneas, escaped. They

8

sailed away and built a new city, Latinum, on the mouth of the river Tiber.

Three hundred years later Numitor was king of this city, but an enemy murdered him and threw his two baby grandsons, Romulus and Remus, into the Tiber. The enemy thought they would be drowned, but a she-wolf found the boys and took them to her cave. Later a shepherd found them in the cave and looked after them until they were grown up. Then they returned to Latinum, killed the murderer, made Numitor's son king and then left to build a new city at the place where they had been thrown into the river. Romulus became king of the city, which was called Rome after him. The new city soon grew into a state which ruled the land around it.

Romulus ruled for many years and five good kings ruled after him. The next king, however, Tarquinius, was so wicked that the Romans drove him out and decided that they would not have any more kings. Instead they set up a republic and chose two men to rule the city state each year. They called these men consuls. To help them rule, a council of wise old men was also chosen which met in the Senate, a building in the middle of the city.

Under the consuls the city grew and prospered. It was in a very good position, being beside a river but far enough from the sea to be safe from pirates. The Romans lived very simply at first, in small houses, and ate plain food. Their dress was a cloak, about ten feet wide, called a toga. This was draped over the left shoulder, down under the right and back up over the left again. Under these togas they wore tunics—a kind of sleeveless shirt. They worked hard to improve their city's buildings and laid down roads all over Italy.

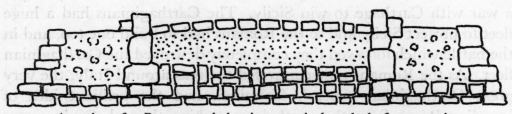

A section of a Roman road showing a typical method of construction

9

The most famous Roman road was the Appian Way which ran from Rome to Brindix.

They built these roads so that their soldiers could march easily all over Italy. These helped them to conquer the neighbouring cities, for the Romans' chief ambition was to make Rome great. Their soldiers were very skilful fighters and soon all Italy from the

Roman soldiers

river Rubicon in the north to Sicily in the south had been conquered. Sicily itself belonged to Carthage, a rival city on the north coast of Africa. This was a challenge to the Romans and soon they began a war with Carthage to win Sicily. The Carthaginians had a huge fleet to protect Sicily and so the Romans had to build one too, and in the battle which followed they completely destroyed the Carthaginian fleet. As the Romans now controlled the seas around Italy, the very great Carthaginian general, Hannibal, had the brilliant idea of invading Rome from the north by marching through Spain across

10

the Pyrenees and Alps and down into Italy. His huge army included elephants. This march was an amazing feat as Hannibal and his army had to climb across mountains covered with snow, for it was in the middle of winter; but, in the end, he was defeated by the Roman general, Scipio, and the wars which were called the Punic wars were over. Rome then attacked and conquered Greece, Macedonia and many other countries to the east including Palestine. Julius Caesar conquered France, which was then called Gaul, and led two expeditions to Britain in 55 B.C. and 54 B.C., whilst another general, Pompey, conquered the Mediterranean countries. Rome was then the master of the known world.

These conquests made Rome a very rich city. Her citizens built

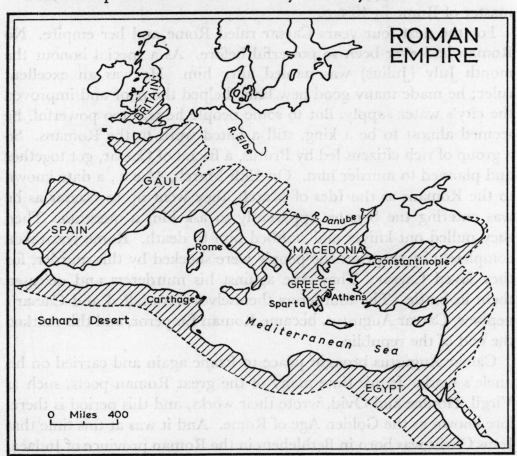

themselves luxury houses and lived very easy and comfortable lives. All the hard work was done by slaves who had been taken prisoner in the many wars the Romans had fought. As Rome was so rich it was very profitable to be elected a consul. Three men were great rivals at this time, Pompey, Caesar and Crassus. They agreed to divide everything between them. Then Crassus, who was already the wealthiest man in Rome, went off to search for some lost gold in Syria, but he was captured by the Parthians who killed him for his greed by melting down gold and pouring it down his throat. This left Pompey and Caesar, but they did not trust each other and finally war broke out between them. Pompey's side lost the war, Pompey himself fled to Egypt, where he was murdered, and Caesar became master of Rome in 48 B.C.

For the next four years Caesar ruled Rome and her empire. No Roman had ever been so powerful before. As a special honour the month July (Julius) was named after him. He was an excellent ruler; he made many good new laws, helped the poor and improved the city's water supply. But to some people he was too powerful, he seemed almost to be a king, still a hated word to the Romans. So a group of rich citizens led by Brutus, a friend of Caesar, got together and planned to murder him. On 15th March, 44 B.C., a date known to the Romans as the Ides of March, they went up to Caesar as he was entering the Senate, apparently to ask him a question. Then they pulled out knives and stabbed him to death. Rome was taken completely by surprise: the people were shocked by this murder, for they loved Caesar. They rose against his murderers and defeated them in battle. The murderers themselves were killed and Caesar's nephew, Caesar Augustus, became Roman Emperor, and this marked the end of the republic.

Caesar Augustus brought peace to Rome again and carried on his uncle's work. In his time many of the great Roman poets, such as Virgil, Horace and Ovid, wrote their works, and this period is therefore known as the Golden Age of Rome. And it was at this time that Jesus Christ was born in Bethlehem in the Roman province of Judaea.

ANCIENT AND ROMAN BRITAIN

2

55 B.C.   Julius Caesar's first invasion of Britain
A.D. 43   Roman Conquest of Britain
A.D. 122—127   Building of Hadrian's Wall

There were people living in Britain for hundreds of years before
the Romans came. The earliest of them were hunters who lived in
caves as near to rivers as they could.
They travelled about in boats on
these rivers, for the country was
covered with thick forests and huge
swamps which made it almost impossible to walk very far. As they
travelled they looked for sharp flint
stones. They needed these to cut
with, for they did not have knives or
anything like that. They made these
flints into axes and cut down trees
with them to make huts to live in
rather than caves. Villages of huts

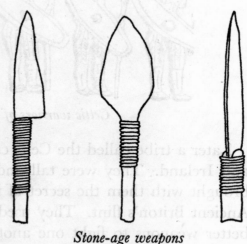

Stone-age weapons

grew up in the clearings in the forests and people in each group of
villages were called a tribe and chose a king or chief to rule over them.

13

These ancient people were mostly farmers who grew food and grazed cattle. They would also hunt for wild animals to kill and eat and they used the animals' skins to make clothes. If they lived by the sea or near a river they would fish. To fish they made themselves very light round boats out of willow branches, with skins on the outside to keep the water out. These boats, called coracles, were very safe, for they hardly ever tipped over even in the roughest sea. Some fishermen in Wales and Ireland still use boats like them today.

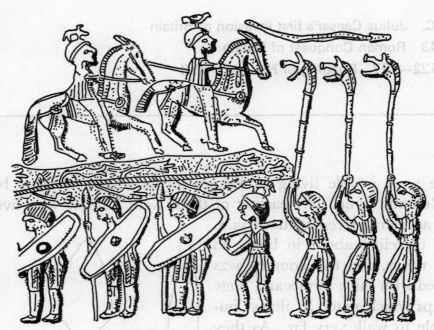

Celtic warriors of the first century B.C.

Later a tribe called the Celts came from Europe to live in Britain and Ireland. They were tall and fair-haired with blue eyes. They brought with them the secret of iron which was far better than the Ancient Briton's flint. They used the iron to make better tools and better weapons to fight one another with, for the tribes were very warlike. One weapon was a war chariot which had curved knives sticking out from its wheels. The Celts came to Britain about six centuries before the birth of Jesus Christ. Dates before the birth of

14

Christ are called B.C. and those after His birth A.D. As they lived before Christ the Celts were of course heathens. They worshipped the Sun and Moon. Their priests, who were called Druids, wore long white robes and taught the people that the oak tree and mistletoe were holy. They sacrificed animals, especially white bulls, and even people to their gods. Most of the Druids lived in Anglesey but they built their altars in other places, such as Stonehenge near Salisbury.

Stonehenge

Very few people dared to sail over the seas away from Britain, for their coracles were not made to stand up to a voyage in the open sea. Nevertheless a few daring sailors did cross the English Channel and trade with their cousins who lived in Gaul, the ancient name for France. They also helped the Gauls against the Romans and this so angered the Roman general, Julius Caesar, that he decided to invade Britain to punish them.

Caesar first invaded Britain in August 55 B.C. At first the Roman soldiers refused to leave their ships for they were terrified by the appearance of the Britons, who had covered themselves with an olive dye and were waiting to fight them on the beach. Finally a standard bearer leapt into the water and waded ashore and the Roman soldiers followed, fearing their standard would be captured. They were too strong for the Britons and soon drove them from the beach. The Britons then asked for peace which Caesar granted them after first having had a brief look inland.

15

Caesar then returned to Gaul, but he came back the next year with a larger army to try to conquer the whole island. He landed near Deal and marched inland. He crossed the Thames at a ford near London and then defeated a large British tribe led by Cassivelaunus which was defending a fort. The Romans captured the fort and built a town around it which they called Verulamium. The Britons again asked for peace and again Caesar granted it to them because he had

Caesar landing in Britain

to return hurriedly to Gaul to put down a rebellion. Before he left he warned the Britons not to help the Gauls again and took hostages from them to make sure they kept their promise. Caesar meant to come back again to finish his conquest but he never had time for he was too busy in Gaul and then in Rome. He wrote, however, an account of his invasions in which he said the population of Britain was very large. The people had plenty of cattle and lived mainly on meat and milk and wore skins. The men had long hair and beards and were fierce fighters.

Julius Caesar was murdered in Rome in 44 B.C., but after a great deal of fighting his nephew Caesar Augustus became emperor. He

16

ruled for forty-four years and after him Tiberius, Caligula and Claudius became emperor in turn. Claudius was determined to conquer Britain, so in A.D. 43 he sent Plautius to Britain with three legions and later came himself. The south was quickly conquered and the Romans immediately built roads so that their soldiers could move easily about the country. The chief road they built was called Watling Street and ran for 259 miles from Deal to London and on up to Chester.

The Britons fought hard, especially those led by Caractacus, but they were steadily driven back into Wales. They were finally defeated in a battle in Shropshire, and although Caractacus escaped from the battlefield he was later betrayed to the Romans and taken to Rome. There, however, he behaved so bravely that Claudius ordered he should not be sold as a slave, but allowed to be free, although he could not return to Britain. Later the Iceni tribe, who lived in Norfolk, rebelled in A.D. 61. Led by their fierce Queen Boadicea, they attacked and destroyed the Roman towns of Colchester, St. Albans and London, killing all the people who lived there. This rebellion was finally crushed by the Roman governor, Paulinus, and Boadicea took poison to avoid being captured.

After this rebellion the Romans decided to attack the Druids, for they were always stirring up the people against Rome. Paulinus therefore led his army across the Menai Straits to Anglesey, and wrecked the island and killed everyone who lived there. Paulinus left Britain after this and Agricola became governor in his place. He was one of the best Roman governors Britain ever had and under his rule the country was peaceful. The only trouble came from the north where the Celtic Picts lived. They were always raiding southwards and to stop this Agricola decided to conquer Scotland. He was very successful there and would undoubtedly have conquered the entire country if he had not been recalled to Rome.

As soon as he had gone the Picts again attacked, so when the Emperor Hadrian visited Britain he ordered a wall to be built along the northern border to keep them out. This wall took seven years to

B

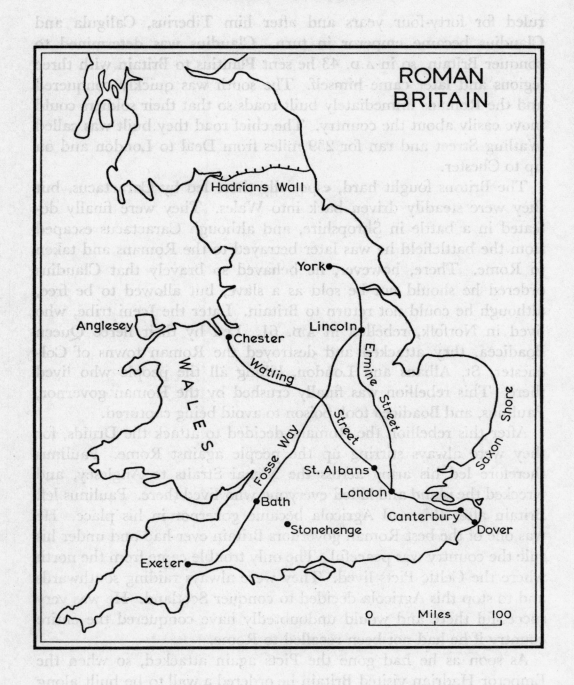

ROMAN BRITAIN

build, but when it was finished it was a magnificent achievement. Seventy-three miles long, it ran from the Solway Firth to the mouth of the river Tyne. It was made of stone, sixteen feet high and eight feet thick. On the northern side a ditch was dug ten feet deep and thirty feet wide. Every five miles there was a fort and every mile a watch tower built into the wall. For years the wall was successful in keeping the Picts out and, although it was later destroyed, parts of it can still be seen today.

The Roman conquest of Britain was now complete. A line drawn between York and Gloucester divided the country into two. East of this line was peaceful and was covered with Roman villas. West of the line lived the Celts and Britons. They would have liked to attack eastwards into Britain, but a long line of Roman forts kept them out.

3

ROMAN BRITAIN AND THE DESTRUCTION OF THE EMPIRE

A.D. 330   Constantinople becomes capital of Roman Empire
A.D. 410   Rome captured by Alaric the Goth
A.D. 476   Rome destroyed by Vandals

Roman Britain was a peaceful and well governed country after Boadicea's rebellion. Roman soldiers protected her people from attacks either by the Picts or from the German tribes who lived across the North Sea. The capital town was St. Albans (Verulamium), but there were many other towns as well, such as York (Eboracum), Chester (Deva) and London (Londinium). York and Chester were garrison towns for the legions defending the north and west, but there were many other forts where Roman soldiers lived, and there too towns grew up. The modern names of many of these towns end in either -chester or -caster, for the Roman word for camp was *castra*.

Apart from London and St. Albans, the towns were really quite small, with perhaps about 2,000 people living in each. But the towns were well built, with wide streets, pavements and gutters. The main centre in each town was the Forum, a public market place, and it was there that the town business was done. Many towns had

20

public baths as well, with hot and cold water, for the Romans believed in keeping themselves clean. Roman baths can still be seen today at Bath in Somerset. Good roads ran between each town and these made it easy for soldiers to move quickly across the country to any place they were needed. The Romans were wonderful road builders. They covered Britain with nearly 7,000 miles of magnificent straight roads, some of which have lasted to the present day.

A gateway at Verulamium

Britain was a province of the Roman Empire and therefore was ruled by a governor appointed by the emperor. A number of officials helped him to rule the country, some of whom were British. These officials and other rich men lived in large country houses called villas. They were magnificent and the owners of them lived very luxuriously. At meals they loaded their tables with food, which they ate reclining on couches, for it was considered very good manners to eat lying down.

The ordinary people lived in the countryside too, but in huts rather than villas. They were farmers, just as their ancestors had been before the Romans came. They grew wheat and corn and kept animals. In fact they grew so much wheat and corn that they

21

were able to ship a lot of it to Gaul and Rome to be sold, and for this reason Britain was known as the "granary of the north". The people used many Roman articles, especially pottery, but they were not allowed to have weapons in case they rebelled. However, they did not need them, for the Romans guarded Britain from attack. This was not really a good thing because the Britons soon forgot how to defend themselves and when the Romans later left the island they were easily conquered by new invaders.

Head of Nero

For a long time the Romans thought they would never leave Britain, but by A.D. 400 the great empire they had conquered had become very weak. This was because Rome was very badly ruled by almost all the emperors who reigned after Caesar Augustus. Caligula, who reigned a few years after Augustus, was half mad. He was also terribly cruel and loved to see people die, but eventually he was murdered. His uncle, Claudius, ruled after him and he did his best to govern properly, but he was poisoned by his wife in order to make her son, Nero, emperor. Nero was a very bad emperor. When Rome caught fire and was almost completely burned down he blamed it on the Christians and made them suffer terribly. He poisoned both his mother and his wife, and murdered so many others that the Senate finally ordered his death. Nero, however, poisoned himself first.

Fortunately for Rome five good emperors ruled next, one of whom was Hadrian. He travelled all over his Empire and improved its defences. His wall built in the north of England was a part of this. When he died the bad times returned. The real trouble was that the army was too powerful. The soldiers could make almost anyone they wanted emperor and, when they tired of him, kill him and replace him by somebody else. The better the emperor the sooner he was murdered, for the soldiers did not want anyone who could control them. Because of this, the Roman Empire just could not be ruled or defended properly, and it was not long before the tribes who lived outside the Empire began to realize this.

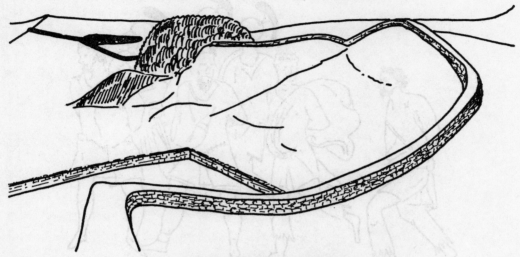

Part of Hadrian's Wall

At last a good man, Constantine, became emperor. He became a Christian and was the first Christian Roman emperor. He was an excellent ruler, and if the emperors who came after his death had been as good the Roman Empire might have been saved. Unfortunately for Rome, they were not. Constantine was determined to rule properly. He realized Rome was too violent a city, so he decided to move away from it and made a new city farther east the capital of the Empire. This new city was called Constantinople after him.

Constantinople was better placed than Rome, for by now the tribes living in the north of Europe were becoming restive. The fiercest of them were the Huns. They began to attack their neighbouring tribes, especially the Goths. To escape, the Goths began to move south into Roman territory. They crossed the Danube in large numbers and defeated a Roman army sent to drive them back.

23

Their leader Alaric realized that the Romans had lost their strength and so he led his tribe far into the Empire. They plundered Greece and then marched on Rome itself. The Romans could not stop them and in 410 Rome was captured. The Goths, however, did not

Gothic prisoners

destroy the city, for Alaric wanted to march south to Sicily to conquer new homes for his tribe. He died, however, of fever before he reached the island.

Rome was now surrounded by enemies. To defend herself she ordered all her soldiers guarding the distant parts of the Empire to return home. But it was too late. The Germanic tribes had seen how easy it was to invade Italy, a far richer and warmer country than theirs, and they began to move south. First came the Huns led by Attila, and, although they were defeated by the Romans and Goths in a desperate battle in 451, another tribe, the Vandals, captured and destroyed Rome in 476.

24

THE COMING OF THE ANGLO-SAXONS

4

A.D. 410   Roman soldiers leave Britain

A.D. 449   The Jutes land in island of Thanet

A.D. 477*c*   Saxon invaders arrive in Britain

At the beginning of the fifth century the barbarian tribes who lived in Northern Gaul and Germany became very restive. Some of these tribes, the Goths, Huns and Vandals, began to move away from their crowded and cold lands towards the warmth and richness of the south, especially Italy. To defend themselves and their cities, the Romans had to recall their troops from such distant parts of their Empire as Britain. The Romans left Britain in 410 and the people were sorry to see them go, for not only had they ruled the country wisely and well but also they had protected it from attacks by the Picts and from other barbarian tribes who lived across the North Sea, such as the Saxons.

The Saxons, who lived in the land between the Elbe and the Rhine, had been raiding Britain for many years even whilst the Romans had occupied the country. They crossed the sea in their long shallow boats to attack the east coast and even sailed up rivers to plunder farther inland. To drive them away the Romans had constructed forts and watch towers all along the coast and had built

25

a fleet of ships. The commander of this fleet was called the Count of the Saxon Shore. When the Romans returned home, however, there was nobody left to protect the country. The Britons themselves had almost forgotten how to fight, for the Romans had not allowed them to have arms during the three hundred years they occupied the island.

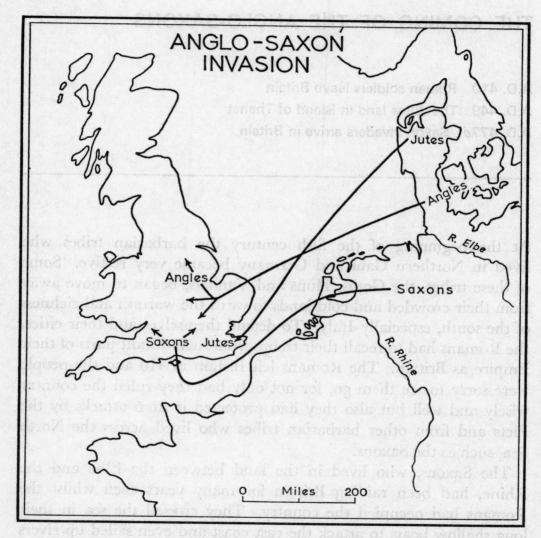

After 410 it did not take long for the Picts and Saxons to realize how easy it was to attack Britain. The Britons put up as good a fight as they could but they were no match for the fierce and often cruel invaders. At last, in 446, Vortigen, the head of a British tribe living in Kent, offered to give a barbarian tribe called the Jutes the island of Thanet in the Thames if they would help him protect his people from the Saxons and Picts. The Jutes accepted, left their lands in Jutland and crossed to Britain led by two chiefs, Hengist and Horsa. For some time they did as Vortigen asked, but they soon realized how weak he was. They found Thanet a far better land than Jutland and so decided to take advantage of Vortigen's weakness to conquer his kingdom. They therefore turned against him, defeated him in battle, and took his lands for themselves. They spread all over the south-east coast of Britain from the mouth of the Thames to the Isle of Wight.

About thirty years later, in 477, the Saxons decided to move across and settle in Britain for they were being attacked in their own lands by the Huns. They landed on the south coast near Selsey Bill and spread all over the area to make the south Saxon kingdom of Sussex. Others of them fought their way farther west to set up a west Saxon kingdom, Wessex, but they were defeated in a battle at Mount Badon by the British and therefore did not spread as far west as they had hoped. These two kingdoms soon became too crowded and so other Saxons pressed inland and set up an east Saxon kingdom, Essex, on the northern side of the Thames beyond the Jutes' kingdom of Kent.

The Jutes and Saxons had thus conquered and settled in the south and south-west of Britain. A third tribe, the Angles, now attacked the midlands and north. The Angles, who came from the Danish peninsula, were probably the most primitive of the barbarians. At first they attacked the lands south of the Wash and conquered them. One tribe settled in the north of this land and another in the south. As the Angles called their people "folk", these parts were called Norfolk and Suffolk. Other Angle tribes pressed inland, sailing easily along many rivers which led from the Wash and driving the British before them. In the midlands they conquered a kingdom they called Mercia and set to work there to clear the forests and drain the marshes. When this land became too crowded another of their tribes attacked northwards, crossed the Humber and won the kingdom of Northumbria.

It took the barbarian invaders about 150 years to conquer their new lands. Those 150 years must have been violent years, but no records were kept of them at the time so they are known as the Dark

Anglo-Saxons at table

Ages. Towards the end of them a new Britain emerged, a Britain divided into seven barbarian kingdoms; Kent, Sussex, Wessex, Essex, East Anglia, Mercia and Northumbria. The Britons had been driven out of their lands and forced into Devon, Cornwall and Wales. For them, these "dark" years were terrible times. Their homes, families and way of life were completely destroyed. But they had their heroes and perhaps, because they had very little else, they praised their heroes a little too much and made up stories about them that were not really true.

28

One of their heroes about whom wonderful stories were later told was King Arthur. The stories claimed that Arthur was king of a western British kingdom. He had a large number of brave and daring knights who rode all over the country in search of the Holy Grail, which meant a vision of God, killing giants and monsters and

King Arthur

rescuing ladies from dragons. They used to meet together with their king at such places as Camelot, Tintagel and Caerleon, and sit around a round table. These are very exciting and charming stories and must have been partly true, though only partly.

What is true is that such a person as Arthur did live at this time, but he was a British battle leader rather than a king. He commanded a troop of cavalry and rode all over the country with it, helping the Britons against the invading barbarians wherever he could, but especially in the west. The invaders did not have cavalry themselves and thus the sudden arrival of Arthur in a battle usually won the battle for the British, and helped to build up later the stories about him. Arthur is believed to have fought in about twelve battles, one of which was Mount Badon. He was, therefore, a captain of mounted soldiers: grateful Britons, who were often saved by him, made him later into a king and his cavalry into knights. As for the stories of giants and dragons, they too were probably invented by the Britons, for no doubt they, who had known peace and security under the

The Round Table

Romans, saw the destructive and cruel barbarian invaders as monsters, giants and even dragons!

There was, however, only one Arthur and many barbarians and so the island was conquered. The Anglo-Saxon conquest was different from that of the Romans. First of all it was much slower and secondly the Anglo-Saxons conquered the land in order to settle down and live on it, whilst the Romans conquered merely to add Britain to their already huge Empire. As they settled down in Britain the barbarians destroyed practically everything Roman. They wrecked the towns

30

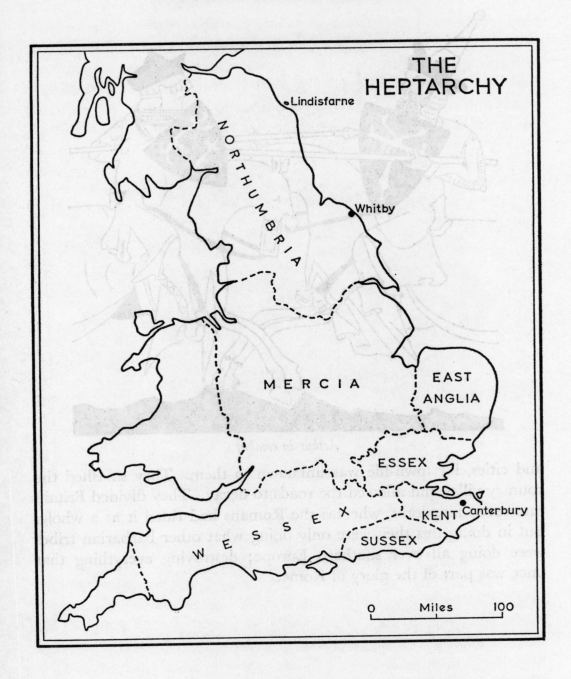

THE HEPTARCHY

Lindisfarne

NORTHUMBRIA

Whitby

MERCIA

EAST ANGLIA

ESSEX

W E S S E X

KENT Canterbury

SUSSEX

0   Miles   100

Arthur in combat

and cities, for town-life was unknown to them. They smashed the country villas and allowed the roads to decay. They divided Britain into seven kingdoms, whereas the Romans had ruled it as a whole. But in doing this they were only doing what other barbarian tribes were doing all over southern Europe; destroying everything that once was part of the glory of Rome.

32

5

THE EARLY CHURCH

A.D. 432   St. Patrick begins his mission to Ireland

A.D. 597   St. Augustine's arrival in England

A.D. 664   Synod of Whitby

The Christian Church which grew up in the Roman Empire in the three centuries after the life of Jesus Christ was persecuted very severely. It was not until the Emperor Constantine became a Christian in 313 that this persecution stopped. Soon afterwards Christianity became the official religion of the Empire and spread to every part of it, including Britain. By then Constantinople was the capital of the Empire, but Rome was recognized as the centre of the Christian religion, and the bishop of Rome was regarded as the head of the Church on earth.

The fifth-century barbarian invasions destroyed the Roman Empire, but not the Christian Church. In fact many of the barbarians were converted and settled down afterwards far more peaceably than they might otherwise have done. Thus Rome, although her Empire was gone, was still regarded as a very important city and the influence of her bishop grew stronger and stronger as more and more barbarians became Christians. In 590 a very great man became bishop of Rome, or pope. He was Gregory I and, because of his work, was afterwards called Gregory the Great. He got everyone to recognize that, as pope, he was head of the Church. He then reorganized and strengthened the Church all over Europe and sent missions to many countries that were still pagan, including Britain.

Britain was not, of course, completely a pagan country, for Christianity had reached the island during the Roman occupation. The Jutes, Angles and Saxons, however, who invaded Britain in the fifth century, were pagans, and when they drove the British into Wales the British took their Church with them. For a long time they refused to have anything to do with the invaders. In Wales, the British or

Celtic clergy

Celtic Church did great work and produced many saints, amongst whom were St. David, the patron saint of Wales, and St. Patrick, Ireland's patron saint.

The Celtic Church was eager to spread Christianity to other Celts, not only in Wales but in Scotland and Ireland. It was St. Patrick who did so much for Ireland. He was not the first to introduce Christianity into that island but there was nothing earlier to compare with his thirty years of wonderful work. Born in western Britain, St. Patrick was captured in a raid by the Picts and taken off to northern Ireland as a slave. Some years later he escaped in a ship which took him to France and, having spent some time in a monastery there, returned home to Britain. He felt a call, however, to go back to Ireland and spread Christianity there, so in 432 he returned to the

34

island. He was very successful and by the time of his death a strong united Church had grown up in Ireland.

St. Patrick had founded a Church with archbishops and bishops, but after his death many monasteries were built and their abbots soon became far more important in their areas than the Irish archbishops and bishops. This was because the archbishops and bishops found it very difficult to travel around the country visiting their people, as thick forests and wide swamps covered the island. The Irish monks were very active; they became famous for their scholarship and for their zeal. Many of them went abroad to spread their faith all over Europe and many monasteries were founded by them outside Ireland. The most famous of these monasteries was perhaps the one founded by St. Columba on the remote island of Iona in the Hebrides.

At the end of the sixth century Christianity was, therefore, firmly rooted in Wales and Ireland, but not in England, for the Celtic Church refused to have anything to do with the first Anglo-Saxon barbarians who had invaded the island and had behaved so cruelly to the British. It was left to the Roman Church to convert them from their paganism. To do so Gregory the Great planned a mission. He would have liked to have gone himself but he was needed in Rome, so he sent in his place Augustine, the prior of a monastery in Rome. St. Augustine set out with forty monks and landed in Kent in 597. He chose Kent because Gregory had told him that Bertha, the wife of the Kent king, Ethelbert, was already a Christian, as she was the daughter of the Christian king of the Franks. Augustine hoped she would persuade her husband to allow him to work in his kingdom and this she did, so that not only did Ethelbert himself and most of his followers become Christians, but the king also arranged for Augustine to be received peacefully in the neighbouring kingdoms of Essex and East Anglia.

Thus Christianity was introduced into south-east England through the help of a woman. Strangely enough it was also introduced into the powerful northern kingdom of Northumbria by a woman, for

Ethelbert's daughter was married to the Northumbrian king, Edwin, and took north with her a priest called Paulinus. Edwin was converted, but, before Christianity could spread very much farther in the north, Edwin was attacked and slain in 633 by the heathen King Penda of Mercia.

Ruins of Lindisfarne

Edwin, however, had become king of Northumbria only by slaying the previous king and driving his two sons, Oswald and Oswy, into exile. They fled to Iona and lived for seventeen years in the monastery where they became sincere Christians. When they heard Edwin was dead they returned to Northumbria, defeated Penda in battle and won the kingdom. Oswald became king and invited Aidan, a monk from Iona, to come to restore Christianity to Northumbria. Aidan came immediately and, true to the Celtic Church tradition, began by building a monastery. This was at Lindisfarne on Holy Island just off the Northumbrian coast. Penda, however, invaded again and killed Oswald in battle and it was not until Oswy, in turn, defeated and killed Penda in 655 that Christianity was safe in

36

Northumbria. Missionaries from Iona and Lindisfarne then spread the gospel to Mercia and south into Wessex.

The Celtic Church had, therefore, done magnificent work in bringing back Christianity to Britain. From Wales it had spread the

A page from the Lindisfarne gospels showing St. Luke

gospel to Ireland, Scotland, Northumbria, Mercia and Wessex— most of the British isles in fact. The Celtic Church had thus done far more than the Roman Church which had converted only south-east England. The Celtic Church, however, was not nearly as well planned as the Roman one. The Roman Church had the pope as a definite head whom all its members obeyed; the Celtic Church had no such one person. The Roman Church had a very good organiza-

37

tion spread over much of Europe and was therefore better able to look after the English Christians than the Celtic missionaries were.

Saxon church tower in Northamptonshire

It was impossible to have the two Churches in the one country for they had many differences. The two Churches had different ideas about baptism, and each Church had its own method of calculating the date of Easter. So it happened in 664 that King Oswy, who belonged to the Celtic Church, was celebrating Easter, while his wife, a member of the Roman Church, was still in the middle of her Lent fast. Oswy realized this muddle could not be allowed to continue, so he called a meeting to decide between the two Churches in his kingdom.

This Church meeting, called a Synod, took place at Whitby in 664 and both Churches sent speakers to it. It was obvious to everyone, however, that Oswy would choose the Roman Church, for it was by far the bigger of the two and, by joining it, Northumbria would link itself with the Christian Church in Europe. Oswy did indeed choose the Roman Church

and although his decision applied only to his kingdom, the rest of England followed his example. For the first time the English Church acknowledged the pope as its head.

6

THE COMING OF THE VIKINGS

A.D. 732   Battle of Tours
A.D. 789   First Viking attack on Britain
A.D. 800   Charlemagne crowned Holy Roman Emperor

By 700 Europe was peaceful again after the violence of the previous three hundred years. The barbarian tribes which had invaded the Roman Empire had settled down in their new homes and many of them had become Christians. As early as 481 the king of the Franks, Clovis, had been converted and from that time the power of the Franks grew. The tribe lived in southern Gaul (France) and had a great deal of influence over other tribes living nearby.

Some two hundred years after Clovis, Charles Martel (nicknamed the Hammer), became ruler of the Franks. He was a great Christian champion and fought many successful wars against heathens. He was especially successful in defeating the Mohammedans at the Battle of Tours in 732 and driving them out of Europe. This victory probably saved Europe from becoming Mohammedan and made the Franks the most powerful tribe in Europe.

In 768 Charles Martel's grandson, Charles the Great, became king. Charlemagne, as he is now called, was one of the greatest kings of medieval Europe. Very tall, strong and agile, he was determined to make himself king of all Europe and to spread the Christian religion as far as possible. He quickly conquered the Saxon tribes who lived to the north of his kingdom, marched into eastern Europe conquering the Slavs and Avars and finally forced the Lombards, who lived in northern Italy, to submit to him. He made every tribe he conquered accept Christianity and built monasteries there to make sure they remained Christian after he himself had gone. Charlemagne's rule now stretched over almost all the old Roman Empire, and so it seemed a good idea to Pope Leo III to offer Charlemagne the title, not just of Emperor, but of Holy Roman Emperor, as Charlemagne was such a good friend of the Christian Church. Charlemagne accepted this title and was crowned by the pope on Christmas Day 800 in St. Peter's Church at Rome.

Clovis, King of the Franks

Charlemagne ruled his huge empire until his death fourteen years later. It was an amazing achievement for one man to rule so successfully over such a large area, but after his death it was impossible to find another one amongst his sons to continue his work. His Empire was, therefore, divided later between his three grandsons. This, of course, greatly weakened the Empire and made it quite unable to defend itself against a wave of attacks by a new North European barbarian people, the Vikings.

The Vikings came from the three North European countries of Norway, Sweden and Denmark, and were therefore also known as the Northmen. They were very fierce warriors; reckless, cruel and heathen. They worshipped their gods of war and thunder and believed that they would go straight to Valhalla, their heaven, to join their gods in endless feasting if they were killed in battle. Wherever they went they inflicted great destruction and misery and caused a historian to record in the Anglo-Saxon Chronicle the prayer, "From the fury of the Northmen, O Lord, deliver us".

Charlemagne

The Vikings attacked by sea, appearing suddenly off the coast in their long narrow sixteen-oared boats with striped sails. Each boat held forty fighting men and at times the Vikings could land armies of up to a thousand wherever they wanted. Their boats were strong enough to sail safely across the open sea and up any river and were light enough to be carried overland if necessary from one river to

41

another. The Northmen sailed their boats all over Europe, raiding every country that had a coastline. The Swedish and Norwegian Vikings attacked Shetland and Orkney, Scotland, the Hebrides, the Isle of Man and Ireland. From 795 onwards they terrorized Ireland until they were defeated by the great king Brian Boru, at the Battle of Contarf in 1014 and driven away for good.

A Viking ship

The Danish Vikings attacked England and northern France, and sailed through the straits of Gibraltar to raid southern France, Spain and Italy. No country was safe from them. They sailed up every important European river to attack inland; four times they sailed up the Seine to sack Paris. There was no known defence against these new tactics of attacks by sea. For protection, therefore, the peasants relied on a local landowner who was rich enough to build a castle to shelter them during Viking attacks, but in return for this protection the peasants had to swear loyalty to this landowner, pay him money, work for him and become "his" men.

England suffered as badly as the rest of Europe. The main targets of each Viking attack were the rich churches and monasteries, and

England had plenty of both. The Vikings would usually arrive off the coast at dusk, attack at night and be gone by morning before a force could be raised against them, for they always avoided battle if they could. Their raids on England began in 789 (an easy date to remember). In 793 they sacked Lindisfarne and other Northumbrian monasteries. They then had to sail farther inland in search of fresh targets. To do this they would arrive off the coast at dusk and sail inland up a river in the dark. They would hide during the following day ready to attack at nightfall, for darkness made them appear

43

Alfred the Great

fiercer and made their escape easier. Sometimes they would round up the local horses, turn themselves into a kind of cavalry and ride around the countryside terrorizing the local people.

The suffering they caused was enormous. Their attacks mainly took place in the summer and autumn just at the time the peasants were trying to scrape a living out of the soil. The destruction of their crops then meant starvation during the next winter and therefore almost certain death. The monasteries and churches were wrecked, as were any towns that were attacked, such as London in 840.

Up to 850 the Vikings were content with raiding England, but after that date they became interested in conquering the country as it was more pleasant to live in than their crowded and cold lands in Scandinavia. In 850, after sacking Canterbury, a Viking army spent the winter on the Isle of Thanet in the Thames. Then in 865 a huge Viking army landed in East Anglia, spent the winter there and began to conquer the country the following year. Northumbria was easily subdued, as was Mercia soon after, and then, in 870, the Great Army, as it was called, moved into the west to attack Wessex. Wessex, too, seemed sure to be conquered to complete a Viking conquest of England, but as it happened that very year a strong warrior became king of Wessex in her hour of need—Alfred, later known as the Great.

7

ALFRED OF WESSEX

A.D. 865   Viking "Great Army" lands in East Anglia
A.D. 871   Battle of Ashdown
A.D. 878   Treaty of Wedmore

Alfred could not have become king of Wessex at a more vital time. A huge Danish army was bearing down, determined to conquer the kingdom as it had conquered the rest of England in the previous five years. If it succeeded in doing so, the whole of England would become a new Danish kingdom and the Christian religion would again be stamped out in the country as it had been four hundred years earlier.

Alfred was quite determined that his kingdom would not be over-run. In 870, the year before he became king, he had fought a number of battles against the Danes, as they neared the boundaries of Wessex, and had defeated part of their army at Ashdown in the Berkshire Downs. His father, Ethelred, had been killed in one of these battles and this made Alfred realize that Wessex was not then strong enough to resist the Danes if they attacked with their whole army. He needed time to plan and improve his defences and so, to gain this time, he offered the Danes a large sum of money to go away and leave Wessex in peace. The Danes accepted this offer mainly because they were impressed by the resistance Wessex put up in 870 and so moved away to look for easier conquests elsewhere in England.

Alfred had brought Wessex five years of peace and he was determined not to waste a moment of them. He realized he needed an

Anglo-Saxon warriors

army, or fyrd as it was called in Anglo-Saxon, as strong and as well trained as the Danish army. The difficulty, however, was that Alfred's army was made up mainly of peasants who needed to be at home in their villages looking after their crops for most of the summer

Anglo-Saxon farmers

and autumn, just the very time the Danes usually attacked. It was possible therefore that Wessex might be invaded when her soldiers were scattered in their villages all over the kingdom. To avoid this, Alfred divided his army into two parts. One part would be with him

46

in camp ready in case of attack, whilst the other would be at home tending the crops. After a few weeks the two parts would change round: thus Alfred always had an army with him in camp and the peasants were able to grow all the food they needed to feed themselves and their families.

Alfred did not want to be caught by a surprise Danish attack and so he built forts, which were called burghs, all around the borders of Wessex. Each burgh had soldiers stationed in it whose job it was to warn the king if a Danish army invaded Wessex near them and to attempt to delay the invaders long enough for Alfred to lead his army against them before they got too far into Wessex. These burghs guarded Wessex against a land attack, but there was also the danger of a surprise invasion by sea, for the Danes had their ships, in which they could move their troops from one part of Wessex to another to attack unexpectedly without Alfred's knowing anything about it until it was too late. To guard against this, Alfred started to build a fleet to defend his coastline. As this took a long time to do, Alfred had only a few ships ready in 876, but by 911 his son had a fleet of over a hundred with which to defend his coast, and for this reason Alfred is known as the founder of the Royal Navy.

Alfred had, therefore, made full use of the five years' peace he had bought in 871 and was ready for the Danes when they attacked again in 876. By this time the Viking "Great Army" had split into two, one part of it settled in Northumbria and the other in Mercia and East Anglia. The Danish warriors living in Mercia and East Anglia were ruled by a chief called Guthrum, and whilst for a time they were prepared to live quietly in their new homes, they became bored after a few years and decided to attack Wessex once again.

Guthrum built two camps for his army, one at Wareham and the other at Exeter. Using these camps as a base he began to attack Wessex, working very closely with a Danish fleet in the English Channel. Alfred and his army, however, were ready for them and easily drove them away until Guthrum launched an attack in the middle of the winter of 878. Alfred was taken completely by surprise,

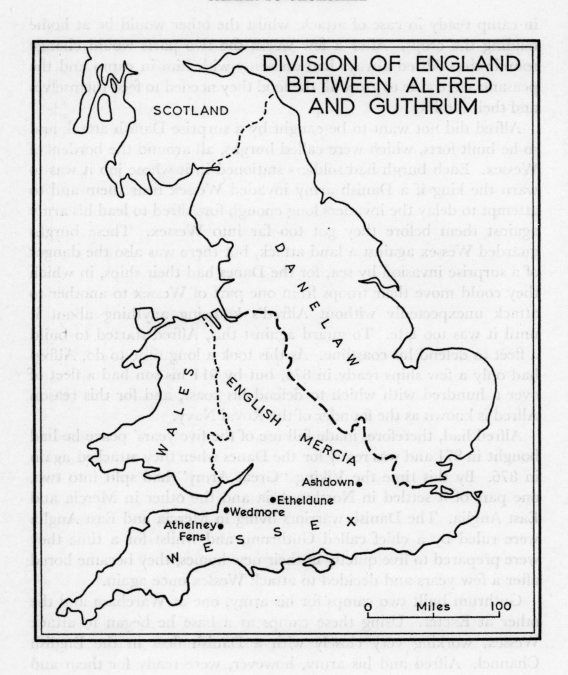

DIVISION OF ENGLAND
BETWEEN ALFRED
AND GUTHRUM

SCOTLAND

DANELAW

WALES

ENGLISH

MERCIA

Ashdown

Etheldune

Wedmore

Athelney

Fens

WESSEX

0   Miles   100

48

for it was most unusual for the Danes to attack at that time. He had to flee for his life and hide in the Athelney fens whilst most of Wessex was overrun. In a few weeks, however, Alfred had gathered his army quietly around him. He then came out of hiding, attacked Guthrum, whose turn it was to be caught by surprise, and completely defeated him at the Battle of Etheldune in Wiltshire. To celebrate this victory, which saved Wessex and England from becoming a heathen Danish

Outline of the Wessex White Horse cut in a hill near Salisbury Plain

kingdom, a white horse was carved in the slope of a chalk hill near the scene of the battle. This white horse, the special sign of Wessex, can still be seen today.

Three weeks later, in June 878, Alfred and Guthrum signed a treaty at Wedmore. By the terms of this treaty the Danes agreed to leave Wessex in peace and to return to their homes in Mercia. Alfred and Guthrum divided England between them, using the old Roman road of Watling Street which ran from London to Chester as a rough dividing line. Alfred was to rule all the country to the south of this line whilst the lands to the north were to be ruled by the Danes and were therefore known as Danelaw. Guthrum also agreed at Wedmore to become a Christian, and he and his warriors were baptized soon afterwards.

Alfred had agreed to divide England between Guthrum and himself, because he knew Wessex was not strong enough to drive the Danes right out of the country. He hoped that one day the kings of Wessex would be strong enough to conquer Danelaw and make

D

themselves kings of all England, and so he determined to spend the rest of his reign working to increase Wessex's strength. His kingdom had suffered very badly from the Danish attacks. Burnt monasteries and churches, ruined villages and untilled fields were common sights. Alfred worked to put all this right and make Wessex a strong and well-ruled Christian kingdom.

The first need was to make sure everyone, whether rich or poor, obeyed the law. As no one was very sure exactly what the law was, Alfred drew up a list of laws, and had them written down and published throughout his kingdom. He also saw to it that anyone who broke the law was properly punished.

The destruction of the monasteries was very serious, for the monasteries were the centres of learning. Alfred realized that uneducated people can never be really happy and so he invited Wessex scholars from far and wide in Britain and Europe to bring education back to his kingdom. He himself founded a school in his palace for his son and for the sons of his noblemen, so that they should be fitted to lead their people when they grew up. He arranged for many classical Latin books to be translated into Anglo-Saxon so that as many of his people as possible could read and enjoy them. He himself had a very inquiring mind. He invented a storm-proof reading lantern, and a method of telling the time by using candles, and his ships were built to his own design. He wrote many letters to important people all over Europe to increase his knowledge of the world. One such person was the Patriarch of Jerusalem who sent him, amongst other things, a suggested cure for the common cold.

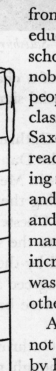

A four-hour candle clock

Alfred died in 900, deeply mourned in Wessex, for not only had he saved his people from the Danes, but by his efforts afterwards he had made Wessex into a great kingdom well fitted to conquer and rule the rest of England.

His son, Edward the Elder, became king after him. He was recognized as king of the English south of Danelaw, but he was determined to increase his authority over as much of Danelaw as possible. His sister, Ethelfleda, married the king of Mercia and this joined Mercia and Wessex together against the Danes. When Edward died Ethelfleda, known as the Lady of the Mercians, carried on his work. The Danes proved difficult to conquer, for they were continually reinforced by warriors either from their old homes in Denmark or from the Danish kingdom in Ireland. In the end, however, Wessex was too strong for them, and by 955 Alfred's grandson, Athelstan, was recognized as king of all the English, and when his son, Edgar, became king the power of Wessex was for a time supreme over all England.

8

THE LAST KINGS OF WESSEX

A.D. 990   Viking attacks begin again on England
A.D. 1002   Massacre of St. Brice's Day
A.D. 1013   Swein conquers England

As king of Wessex, Edgar's power stretched over most of England and he was regarded by almost everyone as king of England. This was because he was strong enough to keep peace in England and protect the people from any possible new Danish attacks. For many years the Danes had kept away from England and those of them who had settled in the country earlier were living peacefully. Then a fierce warrior, Swein, became king of Denmark and began the raids on England all over again.

These attacks began in 990 and within a few years the whole of the south and east coast of England had suffered terribly from them. It was most unfortunate for England that these attacks began again when they did, for Edgar was then dead and his son Ethelred was king in his place. As a king Ethelred was completely useless and, as his nickname of "the Unready" suggests, he was unable to do anything to stop the Danish raids. So he stupidly bribed the Danes to go away, but once they had gone he did not use the time he had gained to prepare his defences as Alfred had done. He did nothing except hope the Danes would not return and when, of course, they did, he was forced to bribe them again. The money the Danes were given to go away was called Danegeld and it was not long before they realized what an easy way it was of making money. They raided again and again and each time demanded more and more money to go away until, finally, they demanded the fantastic sum of 158,000 lb. of silver.

As bribing them clearly did not keep them away, Ethelred tried another method. He gave extra money to some of the warriors to keep the others away but, of course, these warriors merely took the money and did nothing in return. Ethelred was furious at this and, in a fit of temper, ordered that every Dane who was living in England should be murdered on St. Brice's Day, 1002. When Swein heard of this disgraceful deed he determined he would avenge his dead countrymen, especially as his sister was one of the victims. So every year he led ferocious raids on England and ravaged the countryside, so terrifying Ethelred that he fled for safety to the west country and then to Normandy. This left England completely without a leader, so when Swein landed in 1013 with a huge army, the country thought it better to surrender and accept him as king in place of Ethelred than to be savagely destroyed.

Swein, however, died before he could be crowned, and so his son, Canute, became king in his place, although some Englishmen tried to make Ethelred's eldest son, Edmund Ironside, king instead. Edmund, however, died soon afterwards and Canute was then accepted as king by the whole country. He was only twenty-two when he began his reign and within ten years he had also become king of Denmark, Norway and Greenland, but he chose to live in England and rule his huge Scandinavian empire from there.

Unlike his father, Canute was a Christian. He had been converted in Germany and soon showed himself in England to be a sincere believer. At his coronation he promised that he would rule England according to the laws of Wessex and with the help of the Church. He paid his army off and sent most of his warriors back to Denmark,

Canute presenting a golden cross to Winchester Abbey

except for a few whom he kept as a personal bodyguard. To help him control the country he divided it up into earldoms, some of which he gave to his own followers but most of which he gave to Englishmen such as Godwin, whom he made earl of Wessex. He was a very good friend to the Church and did all he could to help it recover from the terrible destruction his countrymen had caused it earlier. He founded new monasteries, gave money to ones already in existence and organized the building of many new churches. In 1027 he went on a pilgrimage to Rome and he chose his chief advisers in England from amongst the archbishops and bishops. Of course he was wise to help and favour the Church, for, in return, the Church supported him and saw that he was obeyed.

There was no doubt that England did very well with Canute as king. He brought peace and order to a country which had suffered terribly in the previous reign from a weak king and violent attacks. It was clear that England would continue to accept him as her king as long as he kept this peace, although he was not an Englishman. But when he died in 1035 his two sons soon showed themselves to be not as good as their father, and so the people of England refused to have either of them as king and instead invited Ethelred's youngest son, Edward, to come back from Normandy where he was living.

Edward was crowned king in 1042 but unfortunately he soon showed himself to be as useless a king as his father. He had been brought up in a monastery in Normandy and he just could not get used to life in the outside world. All his life he remained a monk at heart and, therefore, although he was a well-meaning man and so saintly that he was canonized confessor a hundred years after his death, he was not fitted to be a king. He was far more interested in his plans for building Westminster Abbey than in ruling England, and, in any case, he did not really like the country. He preferred Normandy, where he had spent his boyhood with his Norman cousins.

Edward the Confessor

It was clear that Edward could not give England the strong rule she needed. Ethelred the Unready's reign had shown how fatal it was to have a weak king, so someone had to be found who could help Edward to rule. The earl of Wessex, Godwin, the most powerful man in England, was the obvious man to do this, especially as Edward had married his daughter, thus making Godwin the king's father-in-law. When Godwin died in 1053 his son Harold took his place as the real ruler of England.

Harold Godwinson

Harold was a remarkable man. He was a true Christian, a courageous soldier and a most generous man in peace. He was the king's brother-in-law and had royal Danish blood in his veins. From 1053 to 1066 he ruled England for Edward and seemed to everyone the obvious man to become king when Edward died, for the Confessor had no children of his own. Undoubtedly, Harold too was very keen to become king after Edward.

So when, in January 1066, the Confessor died, on his deathbed

Harold with the Witan

naming, so it was later said, Harold as his heir, Harold immediately claimed he should be king, and persuaded all members of the Witan, the name of a council of all leading Anglo-Saxon men who helped the king to rule the country and who happened to be near London at the time to agree to this. Within a few days he had been crowned king. It is quite clear from all this that Harold was in a great hurry to have himself acknowledged as king in England, although he and most Englishmen regarded it as only right that he should be. The reason for this haste was that he knew he had a rival who also wanted to be king of England. This rival was the Confessor's cousin William, the duke of Normandy. Harold was hoping, of course, that William

56

would give up his hopes to be king of England once he heard that Harold had been crowned, but William was not the sort of man to do this. On the contrary, he was soon making plans to win the kingdom he regarded as rightfully his.

9

THE NORMAN CONQUEST

A.D. 911   Normandy given to Vikings
A.D. 1066   Battle of Stamford Bridge
A.D. 1066   Battle of Hastings

When Edward the Confessor died on 5th January, 1066, Harold was
accepted as king by the whole of England. The claims of William of
Normandy were completely ignored, for nobody in England wanted
a foreigner to rule over them rather than a member of the royal
house of Wessex. William, however, was determined to become
king of England. He had been duke of Normandy since he was eight
years old and now he wanted to add England to the lands he already
ruled. The Normans whom he ruled were descended from the Viking
raiders of the eighth and ninth centuries. France had suffered as
badly as England from their attacks. The worst moment came in
855 when a huge Viking army besieged Paris. Just when it seemed
the city was bound to be captured and destroyed, Odo, the Count
of Paris, came to the rescue and drove the Vikings away. They
settled instead in Normandy in north-west France, along the banks
of the Seine, and finally, in 911, the king of France gave this area to
them to live in for ever on their promising never to attack the rest
of his kingdom again.

William therefore had Viking blood in his veins and thus the excitement of an invasion of England appealed to him. He had known his cousin Edward the Confessor when Edward was living in Normandy before becoming king of England in 1042. Edward greatly admired William and invited him to visit England in 1051. During this visit Edward promised William that when he himself

Harold swearing loyalty to William

died William would be the next king of England. This promise, of course, was not worth very much because Edward later changed his mind and, on his deathbed, named Harold as his heir. In any case, it was not really up to Edward but the Witan to name his successor. None the less, William took this promise very seriously and therefore claimed he was the rightful king of England when he heard of the Confessor's death.

However, by the time the news of Edward's death had reached Normandy, Harold had already been crowned king of England. This greatly angered William, especially as two years earlier Harold had promised him that he would not attempt to become king himself but would help William to become king instead. This promise had been made in William's castle in Normandy where Harold had found himself after he had been shipwrecked on the Normandy coast during a fishing expedition. William had treated him very kindly, but had refused to allow him to go home until he had sworn on holy relics that he would not become king of England when the Confessor died but would help William to do so. Once he was safely home again, Harold said his promise to William did not count as it had been forced and the relics on which he was supposed to have sworn were

Funeral of Edward the Confessor

hidden under a cloth. So, when the Confessor died, he went ahead and became king, especially as it was Edward's dying wish that he should do so.

The crowning of Harold

William, of course, took a different view. He claimed Harold had broken a sacred promise and deserved to be punished for it. He wrote to the pope to tell him of this and added that the English

60

Church was in a very poor condition. He promised the pope he would reform it if the pope would give him permission to invade England. The pope agreed to this and sent William his blessing and a special banner to carry with him to England. This was a great help to William in those superstitious days, for, because of it, many people from outside Normandy joined his army. By September he was ready. His army was well trained and eager to go, the ships to carry it across the fifty miles of open sea were built, all that was now needed was a favourable wind to blow his armada across to England.

In England, meanwhile, Harold had heard William was training an army with which to invade England and was busy preparing his defences. He had gathered his army together and had placed it in position near the south coast ready for William's arrival. Harold, good general that he was, was quite sure William would find it very difficult even to land in England, for he believed his Saxon soldiers would drive the Normans back into the sea as they tried to come ashore from their ships. But suddenly he was faced by an awkward situation in the north. One of his brothers, Tostig, had been expelled from Northumbria several years earlier for disgraceful behaviour. Harold had done nothing to prevent this and for this reason Tostig had a grudge against him. So when he heard that Edward the Confessor was dead and Harold was king in his place, he decided to seek revenge by invading England and trying to drive Harold out. He persuaded Hardrada, the king of Norway, to come with him and together they landed with their armies in Northumbria in early September. There, they captured York and then withdrew seven miles to Stamford Bridge to see what Harold was going to do about it.

It was very difficult for Harold to decide what to do. On the one hand, it was his sworn duty to protect his kingdom from all invaders and he should, therefore, set out north immediately to deal with Tostig and Hardrada. But, on the other hand, if he did take his army north, it would leave his south coast unguarded and make it

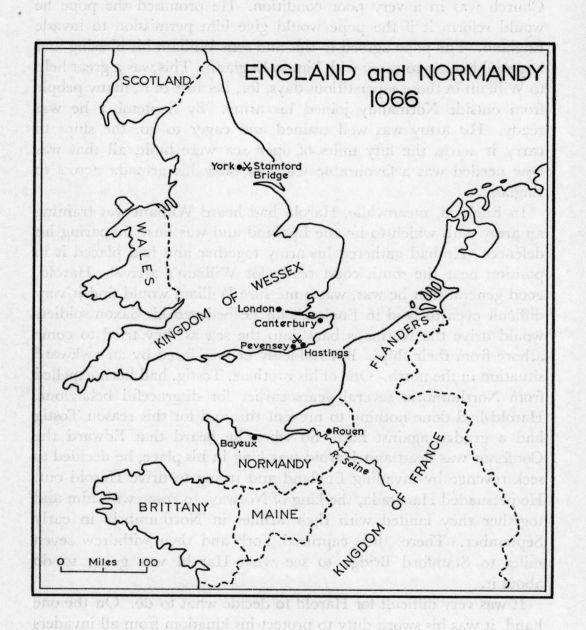

ENGLAND and NORMANDY
1066

SCOTLAND

WALES

York · ✕ Stamford Bridge

KINGDOM OF WESSEX

London ·
Canterbury ·
Pevensey ✕ · Hastings

FLANDERS

· Rouen
Bayeux ·
R. Seine

NORMANDY

KINGDOM OF FRANCE

BRITTANY

MAINE

0   Miles   100

easy for William to cross from Normandy while the Saxon army was fighting in the north. In the end, Harold decided he had to go north and so, hoping William would not get a favourable wind for several weeks, he set off as quickly as he could. Within five days he had reached York, a remarkable achievement. He pressed on immediately to Stamford Bridge where, late at night, he caught the invading armies completely by surprise. Before they could recover he attacked, utterly defeating them. Tostig and Hardrada were both killed and their armies destroyed.

But even as he was resting his victorious army, the news he was dreading reached him. The wind in Normandy had changed in William's favour, he had crossed the Channel with his army and landed safely at Pevensey in Sussex on 28th September, only three days after the Battle of Stamford Bridge. Gathering his tired army Harold hurried south to protect London. On 6th October he reached the city and by 14th October he was in position near Hastings with his army blocking the Norman's path to London. If William wished to advance inland, he would first have to clear the Saxon army out of the way.

William was only too ready to join battle with Harold, for he believed that the only certain way to make himself king of England was to defeat and kill Harold and his family in battle. He knew that he would never be master of England as long as any male member of the house of Wessex was left alive. Therefore Harold need not have hurried so quickly south after the battle of Stamford Bridge, for William would have waited for him near the coast for as long as it was necessary.

The two armies which faced each other on the morning of 14th October were very different. The Saxon army of about 7,000 men was made up mostly of archers and lightly clad soldiers, whereas William's army had, as well, mounted knights on horseback and heavily armoured infantry. Undoubtedly the Norman army, though slightly the smaller, was the better of the two, but Harold had chosen his position with great care, for he had formed up his army on the top of Senlac Hill and this meant that the Norman cavalry would have to charge up a steep slope, a great disadvantage.

The Normans attacked from the very start of the battle but, after six hours of heavy fighting, found they could not break through the solid Saxon front-line. Indeed at one moment a rumour spread through the Norman army that their duke was dead and William had to ride up and down in front of his troops to prove to them that he was still alive. Towards evening William realized that the cavalry would not be able to break the Saxon line as they were finding it

The Battle of Hastings

very difficult to attack up the hill. He decided, therefore, to try an old Norman trick. He ordered his soldiers to pretend to flee and the Saxons, thinking they had won, immediately ran down the slope to pursue the enemy. Once William's cavalry saw the Saxons were on the level ground at the bottom of the hill, they turned round to attack and completely slaughtered them. By the evening the battle was over and Harold's army was scattered. Harold himself was killed by an arrow; all his brothers died with him, and so did every member of his personal bodyguard.

The king was dead and there was no Englishman left with a good claim to become the next king. In these circumstances the country was forced to accept William. He marched to London where he was crowned king of all England on Christmas Day 1066. His victory at Hastings was, therefore, decisive. William realized this and ordered that, as a thanksgiving to God for his victory, an abbey should be built at the top of Senlac Hill on the very spot where Harold fell.

10

THE FIRST NORMAN KINGS

A.D. 1085   Oath of Salisbury
A.D. 1086   Domesday Book
A.D. 1093   Anselm becomes archbishop of Canterbury

As king of England William had far more power than when he was merely duke of Normandy. There were two reasons for this: first, England was a separate country, unlike Normandy which was part of the kingdom of France. The French king was, therefore, king of Normandy and William, as duke, had to recognize that the king was his superior. Secondly, William took over in England all the rights of the Anglo-Saxon kings which gave them the chance to be such strong rulers if they chose to be. William, a masterful man, was determined to make full use of his rights to become a really strong king.

Although he knew the only real reason he was king of England was that he had defeated and killed Harold in battle, he nevertheless claimed he was king because he was the true successor of Edward the Confessor. He persuaded the Witan to agree to this and then arranged to be crowned by an Anglo-Saxon bishop. At his coronation he promised he would rule the country fairly according to English laws. By doing this he hoped that the people of England would

William being offered the English crown

accept him as their king and most of them did. It was not that the people wanted William as king, it was simply that now Harold and his family were dead there was no Englishman left with a better right than William to be king. The common people talked of an English leader called Hereward the Wake who was supposed to be living in the Fen district, but despite this William had very little trouble in England after Hastings and, within six years, he was quite safe as king. Only the north of England rebelled against him and afterwards, as a punishment and a warning to others, William completely devastated a thousand square miles of the countryside there.

One of the first things William had to do in England was to reward his followers who had crossed with him from Normandy. To the most senior of them he gave lands in England for, as king, he claimed to own the whole of England and could therefore do with it as he pleased. He made it clear, however, by charging rent, that the land he gave out was only borrowed from him; he was still the owner. The rent he charged each person for this land was a certain number of knights to serve in the army of five thousand knights he felt he needed to defend England with. Thus a Norman might receive a large estate in return for a hundred knights and that Norman would secure those knights by dividing up in turn part of his land and renting it out to the less powerful Normans who had crossed with William to England in 1066. Each of these men had to promise to serve as a knight in the army for forty days a year in return for his land.

William was careful to see that nobody received too much land in case he raised a large number of knights and became too powerful. He also insisted that all his chief tenants, or barons as they were called, swore an oath of loyalty to him at regular intervals. The Oath of Salisbury, sworn in 1086, was an example of this. He did, however, allow the barons who lived on the Welsh and Scottish borders to have extra knights, for they had to guard England against attacks from the Welsh and Scots. The border area was known as the marches and the barons who lived there as the marcher barons.

68

William ruled England with the help of a small council of friends and relations who were always with him. Three times a year, during the great Church festivals of Christmas, Easter and Whitsun, he held a great meeting which would last for two or three weeks, and to which all the barons had to come. William, who wore his crown

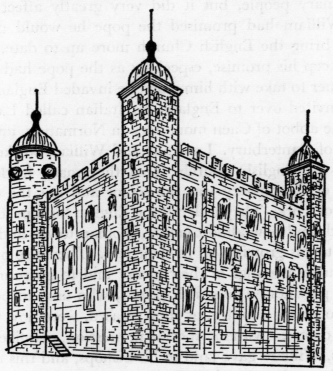

William the Conqueror's Tower of London

at these meetings, discussed the ruling of the country with his barons, who offered him their advice and told him how things were going in their parts of the country. In turn, William would tell the barons anything he wanted done. At the Christmas meeting of 1086, for example, William announced that he wanted an inquiry made to find out exactly how rich everybody was in England and to make sure that no baron was becoming secretly too rich and powerful. Officials were, therefore, sent around the country to collect information which was written down in a special book. As any decision taken by these officials was supposed to last until the end of the world, the day of "doom", this book was called the Domesday book, but, in fact, it was never finished, for William died the following year and his son, William Rufus, was not interested in it.

The Norman Conquest did not make much difference to the lives of the ordinary people, but it did very greatly affect the English Church. William had promised the pope he would make certain changes to bring the English Church more up to date. He had, of course, to keep his promise, especially as the pope had given him a special banner to take with him when he invaded England. William, therefore, invited over to England an Italian called Lanfranc, who was then the abbot of Caen monastery in Normandy, and made him archbishop of Canterbury. Lanfranc and William worked very hard to improve the English Church. First they made it clear that the archbishop of Canterbury was the senior and not the equal of the archbishop of York. They ordered the English bishops to move away from the old, and now almost empty, Roman towns and live instead in the new towns growing up in their sees. They also ordered them to hold regular meetings of their clergy and to go round their sees visiting the parishes. The parish priests, who used to be allowed to wander all over the country, as they pleased, were now forbidden to leave their dioceses without special permission. Unlike the Anglo-Saxon kings, William gave land to his bishops, and this made it very important that only men whom William could trust should be chosen as bishops, for they could use their land, like any other baron, to raise knights against the king. William, therefore, decided who should become bishops, and, although the pope did not now like kings to choose new bishops, Lanfranc was quite happy to allow William to do so, for he knew that, as a sincere Christian, William would choose wisely. When William died fighting in Normandy, however, and his son, the worthless William Rufus, became king in his place, the Church was no longer content to leave such matters to the king, and it was not long before a quarrel broke out.

William II was not the sort of man of whom the Church could

70

approve. Violent, cruel, selfish, greedy for money, he was in many ways a rather bad character. His one real pleasure in life was hunting and he allowed nothing to prevent his getting the greatest possible enjoyment from it. William I had reserved all the forests for himself,

William I and William II. William I is holding a model of Battle Abbey, his son one of Westminster Abbey

but even this was not enough for Rufus. He greatly enlarged them, driving people out of their homes so that the forests could become bigger and bigger. Naturally he soon became very unpopular with the English people for this.

He also quickly became unpopular with the Church. Lanfranc had died in 1089 and William II, instead of immediately choosing a new archbishop, delayed doing so. He did this because as long as there was no archbishop at Canterbury he himself, as king, received all the money that would normally go to the archbishop. It was only when he became very ill in 1093 and feared that he was dying that he chose Anselm as archbishop of Canterbury. William II and

Anselm, however, were such very different people that they could never become as friendly as William I and Lanfranc had been. Anselm, a saint in character, was horrified by Rufus's disgraceful behaviour and chose to go into exile in 1097 rather than live in the same country as such a man. He hoped this would shame Rufus into

Archbishop Anselm

behaving better, but Rufus was not such a man. Instead he was very pleased, for it meant that he could again take the archbishop's money. He found this so profitable that he did not choose new men to succeed the bishops of Winchester and Salisbury when they died but instead kept for himself the money that would have gone to these bishops.

William's greed for money also made him unpopular with the barons. In 1088 there had been a small rebellion against him and finally in 1100 he was killed in a mysterious way. He was out hunting in the New Forest with a group of barons when he was suddenly hit by a stray arrow and fell dead from his horse. Whether this was an accident or murder has never been discovered, but if it was murder, most people would agree that it was no more than he deserved.

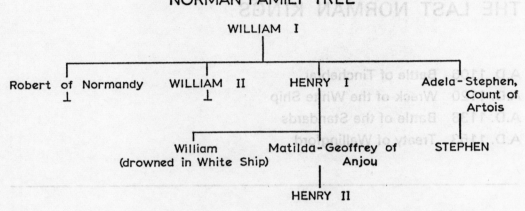

NORMAN FAMILY TREE

E

73

11

THE LAST NORMAN KINGS

A.D. 1106 Battle of Tinchebrai
A.D. 1120 Wreck of the White Ship
A.D. 1138 Battle of the Standards
A.D. 1153 Treaty of Wallingford

William I had ruled both England and Normandy but he ordered that after his death the two kingdoms should be divided between his eldest son, Robert, who should receive Normandy, and his second son, William Rufus, who should rule England. Neither Robert nor Rufus was very pleased with this arrangement, for they would both have liked to rule the two kingdoms, but they had to accept their father's wish.

In 1096 Robert went on the First Crusade, a holy war fought by Christians to try to recapture Jerusalem from the Moslem Turks, and it was whilst Robert was away in the Holy Land that Rufus was killed in the New Forest. By right Robert should now have become king of England but his younger brother Henry had other ideas. He was in England when Rufus was killed, some people say he planned Rufus's death, and he at once seized the royal treasury at Winchester and claimed to be king. The English barons, who had known him for the previous six years while he had been living in

74

England, thought that he would make a good king and so supported him against Robert, whom they hardly knew and whom they considered to be a weak ruler.

Henry knew, however, that Robert would not accept this meekly when he returned from the Crusade. So when three days after Rufus's death he was crowned by the bishop of London (since Anselm was in exile in Rome), he promised his people that he would rule the country fairly according to English laws, keep peace in the land, take no more money than was rightfully due to him and look after the Church. This coronation promise won support for him all over England and so did his marriage soon after to Matilda, a sister of the king of Scotland and a descendant of the royal house of Wessex.

Robert had meanwhile heard of his brother's death and had returned to Normandy from the Crusade. There he was wrongly told that Henry was unpopular in England and all he had to do to become

Robert of Normandy

king instead was to appear in England and the whole country would rally to him. Robert unwisely believed this, crossed to England with a small army, landed at Portsmouth and marched towards London. To his surprise he found he was not at all welcome in England and his army looked very small when he was met by Henry with his army near Alton in Surrey Robert, therefore, did not dare risk a battle but instead had to agree to a treaty by which he promised to return to Normandy and accept Henry as king of England in return for a large sum of money.

Henry realized, however, that he would never be safe as king of England until he had finally dealt with Robert and Normandy, so he decided in turn to invade Normandy. He crossed the Channel in 1106 with an English army and defeated Robert at the Battle of Tinchebrai. He captured Robert at this battle and kept him in honourable captivity in England for the rest of his life, whilst he himself became duke of Normandy in his brother's place as well as remaining king of England.

Twelfth-century ship

Once again, therefore, England and Normandy were joined together, but this meant that Henry had now two countries to rule. He would, therefore, have to spend half his time in each and this made it necessary for him to find a way of ruling each country while he was away from it. To do this he chose a man in each to rule for him while he was away and gave that man almost as much power as he had himself. The man he chose in England was Roger, the bishop of Salisbury, and he called him the king's Justiciar. To keep the peace in England, which he had promised to do at his coronation, Henry sent his own judges around the country to make sure that the local courts were doing their job of punishing wrongdoers properly. This worked so well that it was later said that in Henry's time no man dared harm another, and the king himself was nicknamed "The Lion of Justice".

Henry had also promised to deal fairly with the Church, and so immediately after his coronation he invited Anselm to come back to Canterbury from Rome where he had gone into exile from William II.

76

There was some argument between the two, however, about which of them should choose men to become bishops, but in the end it was agreed that Anselm should choose the men but they would have to swear loyalty to Henry who could object to any if he wanted. Henry

Nightmares of Henry I

was, therefore, still master of the Church, but he did not have as much power over it as his father William I had.

The last years of his thirty-five-year reign were spoilt by the fear that there would be trouble after his death over the choice of the next ruler. Henry had had two children, a son William and a daughter Matilda, but his son was drowned in 1120 when the ship in which he was returning from Normandy, the White Ship, was wrecked off

77

Barfleur. William's death meant that Matilda was Henry's heir, but it was very doubtful if the barons would accept a woman to rule over them and Henry feared they might prefer Stephen of Blois, the son of William I's daughter Adela, instead of his daughter. Henry was determined this should not happen and arranged for Matilda to marry the powerful Geoffrey Plantagenet, the count of Anjou. He also forced the barons twice to swear they would accept Matilda as queen after his own death. When Henry died in Normandy in 1135, however, his plans proved unsuccessful.

It soon became clear that the barons did not want Matilda as their ruler, for though she undoubtedly had the better claim she was a woman and, therefore, most of the barons preferred instead the claims of Stephen of Blois. Stephen had one great advantage which he used with great skill while the barons were hesitating. His brother, Henry, was the very important bishop of Winchester and he was able to persuade his fellow bishops and the two archbishops to support his brother, Stephen, rather than Matilda. When the barons realized the church supported Stephen, they hesitated no longer. Claiming their promise to support Matilda had been forced from them by Henry I and did not therefore count, they accepted Stephen as king.

If Stephen had been as strong a ruler as Henry I he would have had no further trouble in his reign and Matilda would soon have been forgotten. Unfortunately, however, although he had great charm, he soon showed himself to be a very weak king who could neither keep order in England nor defend the country from outside attacks. The Scots continually raided the north, and when finally they were defeated in 1138 at the Battle of the Standards and driven out, it was not the king but the aged archbishop of York who led the English troops. The barons began to lose their respect for Stephen and do more or less as they pleased in their own parts of the country, some of them behaving very cruelly towards the ordinary people. When Stephen foolishly quarrelled with the bishops, his chief supporters, Matilda crossed over to England from Anjou with her chief supporter the earl of Gloucester, to see what advantage they could take of Stephen's difficulties. They made their headquarters in the west of England and for two years watched the king grow weaker and weaker. Then in 1141 they attacked, defeated the royal army at the Battle of Lincoln, and captured Stephen himself. They imprisoned him at Bristol and then persuaded an assembly of bishops at Winchester, including the king's brother, Bishop Henry himself, to declare Stephen no longer king and elect Matilda as queen in his place.

Warrior and battle axe

Matilda, however, was no better at ruling England than Stephen. Proud and haughty, she quickly made herself very unpopular and was driven out of London. The bishops soon regretted their hasty action and turned back to support Stephen once again. Soon afterwards the earl of Gloucester was captured and exchanged for Stephen and this was followed by a long period of fighting between the two sides. Finally, in 1153, Matilda's son Henry, count of Anjou since his father's death in 1151, crossed to England with an army and forced Stephen to agree to a peace treaty at Wallingford. By this treaty it was decided that Stephen should be king for as long as he lived, but when he died Matilda's son, not his, should be the next king. Stephen really gave in at Wallingford but he was an old man by then and was no longer interested in continuing the struggle, for his son, Eustace, whom he had hoped would become king after him, was already dead. The Treaty of Wallingford, therefore, settled the civil war which had dragged on for eighteen years and caused chaos in the country. The news was greeted with delight all over England by the people who had suffered very greatly from the war. The people hoped now for the rule of a strong king who would bring peace and order to the country once again. As it happened they had only one year to wait. Prince Henry, Matilda's son, helped Stephen to rule the country and, when Stephen died a year later in 1154, he became Henry II, the first of a long line of Plantagenet kings.

Warrior and battle axe

12

THE STORY SO FAR

More than twelve hundred years before Henry Plantagenet crossed from Normandy to England to force Stephen to agree at Wallingford that he, as Matilda's son, should become the next king of England, Julius Caesar had crossed, too, from Normandy to try to make himself the ruler of the Ancient Britons on behalf of Rome. Caesar did not, in fact, conquer Britain, because he became too busy in Rome, but between his two visits to Britain and Henry Plantagenet's arrival, the country was conquered on four occasions, first by the Romans in A.D. 43, then during the years around A.D. 430 by the Angles, Jutes and Saxons, next by the Danish Vikings from 1013 to 1042, and finally in 1066 by the Normans.

Caesar had found Ancient Britain to be a country divided up between many tribes which were quite separate from each other. This was still the same in A.D. 43 when the Emperor Claudius sent an army to conquer Britain and, for this reason, had little difficulty in defeating the Britons. Once they had conquered Britain, the Romans ruled it as a whole and thus from as early a date as the first century A.D., Britain was a united country and not one divided up into little parts. The Romans ruled Britain for nearly four hundred years, bringing peace and order to the country, covering it with wonderful buildings and fine roads and defending the people from attacks from Scotland and Europe. Unfortunately the Romans did not allow the Ancient Britons to have arms or to practise using them, so, when the Romans left the country in 410 (the year that Rome was captured by Alaric the Goth) to defend, unsuccessfully as it turned out, their own homeland from attacks by such tribes as the Goths and Huns, the Ancient Britons were unable to defend their homes against another group of invaders from Europe. Between 430 and 550 Britain was attacked and conquered by the Angles, Jutes and Saxons, North European barbarian tribes who were seeking new lands to settle in away from their own cold and crowded homeland.

The period of the Anglo-Saxon conquest is known as the Dark Ages, "dark" because very little is known today of what actually happened during a period of nearly two hundred years after A.D. 430. But at the end of it Britain was divided into three main kingdoms, Northumbria, Mercia and Wessex. There is also no doubt that the Celtic Christian Church was very active in Wales, Ireland and Scotland at this time, as well as in northern England. So when Pope Gregory the Great sent St. Augustine on a mission to England in 597, most people in England were already Christians. The Christian Church became very strong in Britain, especially after the differences between the Celtic and Roman forms of Christianity were settled at Whitby in 664, but then a new wave of barbarian invaders ruined the peace of the country. From 789 onwards the Vikings began to raid England, seeking to steal and destroy what they could. At first they were merely raiders but after 860 they became conquerors as well. A great army of warriors began a determined conquest of England led by their chief, Guthrum. Northumbria and Mercia were easily conquered but Wessex produced in her hour of need a great leader Alfred the Great, who not only saved Wessex at the time from the Vikings but afterwards so organized his kingdom that her later kings were able to win back the rest of England from the Vikings and make the kings of Wessex also the rulers of England.

Unfortunately, two of the last kings of Wessex, Ethelred the Unready and Edward the Confessor, had not the ability to rule England well. Ethelred lost his kingdom to the third conquerors, the

82

Danes, led first by Swein and then by Swein's son, Canute. Edward the Confessor's weakness was the main cause of the successful invasion and conquest of England in 1066 by his cousin William, duke of Normandy, which Harold, the last of the Saxon kings, could not prevent. The fourth conquerors of England, the Normans, like the Romans, ruled the country as one kingdom. Two of the first three Norman kings, William I and Henry I, were very powerful men who were greatly admired both in England and Europe. Their rule made very little difference to the lives of the ordinary people, although their rulers were different, but the Church was very greatly affected by it. William and his archbishop, Lanfranc, introduced several changes to it which were by then practised in Europe and, for the first time, the bishops became great landowners.

The last Norman king, Stephen, though a charming and generous man, was not a good ruler and he could not keep order in England. Civil war broke out between him and Matilda, the daughter of Henry I, whom the barons had refused to have as their ruler as she was a woman and also because they disliked her proud and haughty manner. This civil war, which caused great suffering in England, dragged on for many years until Stephen, on the death of his son Eustace, agreed to accept as his heir Matilda's son, Henry Plantagenet, at the Treaty of Wallingford in 1153. Stephen died the following year and Henry then became king. He was to prove himself one of the greatest kings that England ever had.

When it happened

B.C.

356–323	Life of Alexander the Great
216	Hannibal's invasion of Rome
55	Julius Caesar's first invasion of Britain
44	Murder of Julius Caesar

A.D.

43	Roman Conquest of Britain
122–127	Building of Hadrian's Wall
330	Constantinople becomes capital of Roman Empire
410	Roman soldiers leave Britain
410	Rome captured by Alaric the Goth
432	St. Patrick begins his mission to Ireland
449	The Jutes land in the island of Thanet
476	Rome destroyed by Vandals
477	Saxon invaders arrive in Britain
597	St. Augustine's mission to England
664	Synod of Whitby
732	Battle of Tours
789	First Viking attack on Britain
800	Charlemagne crowned Holy Roman Emperor
865	Viking "Great Army" lands in East Anglia
871	Battle of Ashdown
878	Treaty of Wedmore
911	Normandy given to Vikings
990	Viking attacks begin again on England
1002	Massacre of St. Brice's Day
1013	Swein conquers England
1066	Battle of Stamford Bridge
1066	Battle of Hastings
1085	Oath of Salisbury
1093	Anselm becomes archbishop of Canterbury
1106	Battle of Tinchebrai
1120	Wreck of the White Ship
1138	Battle of the Standards
1153	Treaty of Wallingford

Kings of Wessex and England

Alfred the Great	871–900
Canute	1014–1035
Edward the Confessor	1042–1066
Harold	1066
William I	1066–1087
William II	1087–1100
Henry I	1100–1135
Stephen	1135–1154